Original title:
Life's Purpose: Still Under Construction

Copyright © 2025 Creative Arts Management OÜ
All rights reserved.

Author: Liam Sterling
ISBN HARDBACK: 978-1-80566-114-6
ISBN PAPERBACK: 978-1-80566-409-3

Scribbles of Serendipity

In a world of tangled strings,
I dance on whims and silly things.
With plans that twist like pretzel shapes,
I chuckle at my awkward scrapes.

A roadmap drawn with crayons bright,
Leads to the wrong turn every night.
I bake my dreams like gooey pies,
And serve them with a side of fries.

Each goal a puzzle with missing parts,
My compass spins, but here's my arts!
With laughter echoing off the walls,
I trip on purpose, then do the rolls.

So grab a spoon, let's dig right in,
To find the mess that's where we've been.
For life is wildly out of breath,
And purpose? Oh, it's out to test!

Half-Built Roads and Open Sky

A road that twists, a bridge not done,
Weaving laughter under the blazing sun.
Potholes dip into plans gone awry,
Yet here we skip, with a wink to the sky.

Tools and beams scattered all around,
A hammer sings, a joyful sound.
We trip and fall, then rise with cheer,
The destination can wait, let's have a beer!

Journeys in Progress

Packing bags, a mess of socks,
Maps crumpled up, ticked by the clocks.
Each step I take, a brand-new riddle,
Still, I dance on this unplayed fiddle.

Wanderlust? More like wander what's next!
Caught in delays and minor perplexed.
But every stop is a show with a snack,
Promising joy, reminding me to slack.

Threads of Intent Unraveled

Knots of thought, a tangled yarn,
Intentions meander, creating a barn.
A stitch here, a thread there,
Oops, now I've knitted a fluffy bear!

Plans unravel like old school pranks,
Each twist reveals a spiral of thanks.
The fabric of dreams, a patchwork surprise,
Stitching giggles under open skies.

The Art of Becoming

A sculptor chips away, what a sight,
Finding form in the morning light.
Molded clay, yet still so odd,
Is that a figure or just a fraud?

With every stroke, I'm redefining me,
Halfway to genius, just wait and see!
Laughing at the mess and the clay in the air,
Maybe it's art? Perhaps I'll declare!

The Ongoing Journey of Becoming

I'm building my path, but it's quite a mess,
With bricks of laughter and goals in distress.
Every step I take, I trip on my dreams,
Like chasing shadows or sliding on cream.

I'm supposed to be wise, but I can't find my socks,
Navigating through life in flip-flops and Crocs.
Construction's a problem, delays never cease,
Yet I dance through the chaos, searching for peace.

In Progress: A Personal Odyssey

I set out with plans, but I'm lost on my street,
Maps full of doodles, my thoughts can't compete.
I'll follow the signs, but the signs are quite silly,
   Like 'Free Ice Cream' and 'Danger: A Milly'.

My odyssey's painted with crayon and cheer,
Where every wrong turn is just part of the gear.
With a wink and a nod, I'll embrace the absurd,
   After all, who owns the 'right' or the 'heard'?

Paths Being Carved

I wander through forests where squirrels take charge,
Their chatter like life tips, all covered in large.
With axes of humor, I carve out my way,
Chasing each feather, come what may.

Turning each corner, I meet with surprise,
The path I thought ready, a jest in disguise.
I'll giggle with trees like they know my plight,
As I forge my own route beneath starlit night.

Paints and Particles of Possibility

Armed with my brush, I'm a painter of fun,
With splashes of chaos, oh look, there's the sun!
Each color I mix drips on life's grand floor,
A masterpiece messy, yet I keep wanting more.

I splash on my goals, with a twirl and a twist,
Adding in sparkles, can't let them be missed.
The canvas of 'now' is alive with delight,
In this gallery's make-shift, I'll dance into night.

Shaping Shadows into Light

In a world of hammers and nails,
We build our dreams with giggles and gales.
Chasing visions while tripping on shoes,
Each misstep is a story to choose.

Blueprints tangled like my morning hair,
Guiding me through this comedic affair.
Laughter echoes where doubts used to dwell,
As shadows transform into jokes we can tell.

Scaffolding of the Soul

A ladder to nowhere, or is it to fun?
We balance our hopes in the rays of the sun.
Each rung I climb wobbles, then shakes,
Yet up I go, with each little quake.

Nailed with dreams that sometimes fall flat,
I patch the gaps with a laugh and a chat.
Wobbling still, like a popcorn machine,
I build my spirit, if only my spleen!

Patchwork of Aspirations

Cut and stitch with colors quite bold,
Every fabric tells stories untold.
A patch here, a patch there, oh what a sight,
Creating a quilt that's cozy and bright.

Some patches are messy, while others align,
But together they make a pattern so fine.
With each quirky shape, a belly laugh brings,
The joy in the chaos, oh what laughter sings!

Navigating the Labyrinth of Hope

A maze of ideas, I twist and I turn,
Following whims with a voracious yearn.
With signs that say 'lost' but laughter says 'go',
I dance through the turns, stealing each show.

Minotaurs lurking? Just cardboard and glue!
Imagining monsters, but what can they do?
With each twist of fate, a silly surprise,
Navigating my dreams with wide-open eyes.

Seeds of Possibility

In the garden of dreams, we plant with glee,
Hoping for flowers, though weeds come for tea.
Watering doubts like they're precious gold,
Nature laughs hard at plans that we hold.

Sprouting ambitions, some tall, some short,
Trying to harvest a grand life report.
But the critters come nibbling, oh what a plight,
This comedy of errors keeps us up at night.

A Canvas Unrolled

I unroll my canvas with colors so bright,
Slapping some paint in a glorious fright.
Strokes of confusion, splatters of cheer,
Turns out my masterpiece's nowhere near.

Each day is a brush, each choice a hue,
Swirling together like a quirky stew.
In the gallery of laughter, there's no strict review,
Just a mix of chaos and dreams overdue.

The Architecture of Change

Building a tower of hopes and of schemes,
Using duct tape, some pasta, and dreams.
Blueprints in crayon, this structure may sway,
Yet laughter holds up what plans would betray.

Constructing new paths with Lego and glue,
Hope the foundation holds—so far, so true!
With every misstep and wobble I face,
I'm crafting a palace of messy grace.

Paths Yet to Wander

With a map full of doodles and signs of confusion,
I wander the world like it's all an illusion.
Each turn leads to laughter, each road brings a grin,
Who knew getting lost could feel like a win?

Chasing the sunsets with socks that don't match,
Every stumble just adds to my catchy new batch.
Some say I'm silly, I shrug with a smile,
These are my journeys—I'll linger a while.

The Unseen Hands Behind Tomorrow

Woke up today, looked around,
Sneezing hard, I hit the ground.
Thought I had a plan, oh dear,
Turns out, I just lost my beer.

Juggling dreams and socks, I swear,
Is that a ghost, or just the air?
Building castles in the sand,
I'll take my time, just wave my hand.

Life's a puzzle, no one knows,
Where it ends or how it goes.
I'll pave the way with silly strings,
And dance around like I'm the king.

So here's to plans drawn in the sky,
With clouds that dance and birds that fly.
Each twist and turn feels quite absurd,
But I'm no fool, I chose this word.

Open Canvas

With brushes made of spaghetti,
I'll paint the world, though it's all messy.
Each stroke a giggle, each shade a prank,
What's wrong with purple? Give it a flank!

A canvas bare and all untamed,
Paint splatters here, nothing's the same.
Each corner holds a dream or two,
Oh look! There's my shoe – in bright blue!

As I mix these colors bold,
My masterpiece starts to unfold.
A flamingo dances on my page,
While I munch chips, the latest rage.

What's the rush? I'll take my time,
With every dash, I make a rhyme.
In this chaos, I will roam free,
Creating laughter, just wait and see.

Unfinished Masterpiece

A statue waits, no arms or legs,
Shaped like a chicken, quirky pegs.
Every day it sighs and leans,
Dreams of being more than beans.

It's not done, no need to fret,
Who needs a face? I'll place a pet.
A turtle's hat, a fish-shaped shoe,
This world's so silly, who knew?

The sculptor laughs, he's taking breaks,
While sipping tea and plotting fakes.
The masterpiece is far from clear,
But what a joy to keep it near!

So here's to art that feels all wrong,
Each brushstroke sings a funny song.
In this chaos of clay and bits,
I'm not alone, it surely fits.

Echoes of What Could Be

I hear them whisper in the night,
Those dreams that dance away from sight.
"Try again!" they giggle and tease,
While I search for lost car keys.

Future plans like noodles bend,
Twist and curl, they never end.
But maybe that's their special charm,
A life of chaos, oh so warm!

Like echoes bouncing off the walls,
They laugh and stumble, share their calls.
No need for straight lines when they roam,
Each wayward path can still feel home.

So here I go, a whimsical maze,
With giggling dreams, my heart ablaze.
Embrace the mess, let laughter fly,
In this wild ride, together we try.

The Evolving Sketch of We

Doodle squiggles on a page,
What a wonder, what a stage.
Each line a story, not in stone,
With laughter ringing, we're not alone.

Like wobbly bikes with no two wheels,
We ride through life, no grand ideals.
But joy erupts from simple things,
Like cupcakes, cats, and colorful rings.

With flip-flops flopping, here we go,
Sketching moments, row by row.
A little wobbly, but that's our flair,
Life's a circus, a clown's affair.

So grab your crayon, let's create,
No deadlines here, just giggles await.
In this evolving dance, we sway,
Together forever, come what may.

The Layers Beneath the Surface

In the mirror, I find a grin,
With a hat of dreams and a shirt of sin.
Peeling back layers, oh what a sight,
Like an onion crying, I'm quite the fright.

Underneath the chaos, plans go astray,
Sketching on napkins, I'm lost in the fray.
A life of laughter, bumps, and cheers,
I'll figure it out while sipping my beers.

Puzzles and riddles, I dance with fate,
Chasing my tail, there's no time to wait.
Who needs a map when you've got a song?
Hum along and you can't go wrong.

As the paint peels and the woodwork sighs,
I just add another coat, oh what a surprise!
Construction's messy, but I make it fun,
With a wink and a nod, I'll get it done!

Open Ended Expressions

My canvas is blank, but I'm never out,
With crayons of wisdom, I scribble about.
A dash of chaos, a sprinkle of glee,
Each stroke a question, who will I be?

Coffee cup puddles, they spill on the floor,
Like my thoughts leaking, oh what a chore!
Pants inside out, but hey, who's to judge?
I wear my life like a festive grudge.

With dreams like balloons, I drift toward the sky,
Tethered by laughter, I'm not asking why.
Open-ended chapters, no time to fret,
Life's just a party, no room for regret.

So here's to the scribbles, the doodles galore,
Each misstep a dance, each fumble a score.
I raise my glass high, cheers to the jest,
In this crazy ride, I'm truly blessed!

The Unfinished Narrative

With chapters misplaced, I'm lost in the tale,
Characters bouncing, some tell a big fail.
My plot twists like spaghetti, oh, what a mess,
But I can't help but giggle, I must confess.

Notes in the margins, thoughts on the fly,
Every page is a circus, just give it a try.
My protagonist stumbles, meets silly fate,
They trip on a banana, it's never too late.

Each paragraph's bloated, with ink drips and stains,
Confetti of nonsense courses through my veins.
A dash of whimsy, a scoop of odd grace,
I'm crafting my story, it's all a big race.

So if you read on, please lower your guard,
Plot holes may pop up, some might leave you jarred.
But with laughter as glue and absurdity's spark,
I'll finish this journey and leave my mark!

Dreams Under Renovation

A house full of dreams, the blueprint's unclear,
Nails popping out like my thoughts, oh dear!
The ceiling's a canopy of hopes and dashed rhymes,
But I dance through the dust, creating new times.

With a hammer and wish, I patch up the seams,
Bolts of enthusiasm holding up schemes.
A staircase to nowhere, how could it be?
I'll slide down the banister, wild and free!

Paint chipping away, but I'll slap on a coat,
Brighter than moods, they're like songs I wrote.
Sawdust and laughter, that's how I roll,
Building my castle, it's good for the soul.

In this quirky abode, where dreams are aglow,
I'll keep adding stories, come join in the show!
With laughter as currency, I'm never alone,
In this house of misfits, I've found my home!

Sculpting the Unknown

With chisel in hand, I take my aim,
To carve out laughter, but it's quite a game.
What once was a block, is now quite bizarre,
A duck with a top hat? Now that's gone too far!

Each chip that falls dances to the floor,
As I shape a vision that leaves me wanting more.
If I could just find the manual's page,
I might just create a wise old sage!

My masterpiece calls, yet it wiggles away,
A salad of dreams in a whimsical play.
I sculpt for the joy, not just for the fame,
Yet some say my art looks a bit like a game!

So I'll keep whittling through laughter and cheer,
With each silly piece, I conquer my fear.
In this quirky saga where laughter takes hold,
I mold a tomorrow both funny and bold!

Footprints on a Fresh Page

A blank sheet of paper, oh what a sight!
No rules or maps, just daydreams in flight.
I scribble my thoughts like a toddler with glee,
Each line's a wild dance, come join me, let's be!

Ink blots like hiccups, they splash and they spew,
As I ponder if ducks might just wear a shoe.
From honeybee buzz to a cat's silly prance,
Every silly doodle is a chance to romance!

But wait, what's that flutter? A paper-made boat!
It sailed from the edge, oh what a good note!
As I chase after mischief, my pen got away,
Now it's veered off course in a chuckle-filled sway!

Yet through this chaos, a message rings true,
Each footprint of ink whispers, "Just be you!"
So, I celebrate blunders, with smiles I'll engage,
For life's a grand journal, my fresh open page!

Blueprints of Tomorrow

With a pencil in hand, I sketch out my fate,
A rollercoaster ride, oh wouldn't that be great?
I draw in some clouds; maybe some rain,
And a giant hot dog stand—can't have too much gain!

These blueprints are wild, with twists and with turns,
A few surprising tunnels where laughter just churns.
I slopped down some colors, the shades are a riot,
A rainbow of chaos—yup, I can't deny it!

As I glance at my plans, they start to wiggle,
Like they had too much candy, it's time for a giggle!
My dreams on this page won't neatly confine,
They dance and they prance like a jiggly line!

I lift my eyes high, towards horizons way wide,
Where fun meets adventure—I jump at the ride!
So here's to the chaos, and dancing in light,
In these blueprints of whimsy, tomorrow feels bright!

Building Dreams from Dust

With a shovel in hand, I start from the ground,
Each grain of old hope is a treasure I've found.
I toss up a castle, oh wait, it's a chair,
Who knew my ambitions would breathe in the air?

Dust bunnies scatter, they've joined in the fun,
They giggle like mad, as the last piece is done.
From dust comes a dragon, or maybe a kite,
If laughter's the goal, then it's surely alright!

My tools are all quirky, a spoon and a fork,
I build with those gadgets and maybe a cork.
From glittering dreams to some rather weird plans,
I construct joyful things, with my makeshift hands!

So here's to my venture, both nutty and bright,
A world made of laughter, where jokes are the light.
With dust as my canvas, I cheerfully trust,
That building up wonders is truly a must!

Chasing Shadows of Fulfillment

I chased a shadow in the sun,
It giggled and it tried to run.
I tripped on dreams, fell on my face,
Turns out 'fulfillment' loves to race.

With maps in hand, I took a stroll,
Through puddles deep and rock 'n' roll.
I asked my cat, 'What's next to do?'
He curled and snoozed—didn't have a clue.

I climbed the tallest tree around,
To yell my thoughts, but lost my sound.
"Hey universe, are you awake?"
It just chuckled, "Make no mistake!"

So while I'm stalking my big goals,
I'll dance with daisies, do silly roles.
For laughter makes the journey bright,
And I'll keep running, day and night.

Tapestry of Intentions

I wove a tapestry with care,
But oops! I snagged it on a chair.
Each thread of joy, each tug of fate,
Was mixed with donuts on my plate.

Intentions sprout like weeds in spring,
With all the nonsense they can bring.
A llama told me, "Be a friend,"
Yet all I heard was "Chase the trend."

My needle's blunt, my fabric's torn,
I stitched a smile, but it's all worn.
With laughter thread, I'll patch it tight,
And wear my blunders with delight.

I'll flip the fabric inside out,
Dance with the quirks, scream and shout.
A masterpiece or just a mess?
It's all a joke—I must confess!

Bridges Yet to Build

I started sketching out some plans,
But all I drew were wiggly hands.
With beams of hope and nails of fun,
I'll build a bridge, or maybe none.

Each plank's a wish, a crazy dream,
Like jellybeans in a sunlit stream.
They ask me how, I just respond,
"Maybe later," and then I yawned.

I trip on blueprints laid about,
Laughing loud, with doubts that shout.
A tugboat told me, "Grab a snack,"
As if that's all I need—no lack!

So while the bridges sway and quake,
I'll dance with chaos, for my sake.
A journey's worth, no map in sight,
I'll go on building, day and night.

Whispers of the Future

I heard the future call my name,
But ended up playing a silly game.
It whispered secrets soft and low,
While I just wanted pizza dough.

Dreams tiptoed through my cluttered room,
With wild ideas that made me zoom.
A squirrel once winked, said, "Just relax,"
While I fell over my snack-stash cracks.

I pictured glories, shiny and bright,
But then got caught up in a pillow fight.
The whispers laughed, "What's your next plan?"
I shrugged, said, "Maybe a magic van."

So here I am, still in a daze,
Floating through laughter's goofy maze.
While visions twirl, I'll join the spree,
For life's a jest, as fun can be!

Hammers and Hopes

Nailed a dream, hit my toe,
Now I dance, but move slow.
With a grin and a sigh,
I'll build my tower to the sky.

Screws are loose, the plans askew,
But laughter's my favorite glue.
Each misstep, a chuckle or two,
Crafting joy's what I'll pursue.

Paint it bright, splash of love,
With a dash of "oops" from above.
In this messy work of art,
Every flaw plays a part.

So grab a tool, let's fix the scene,
With silly hats, we're the dream team.
In the chaos, we find our way,
Hammers and hopes save the day.

The Unwritten Script of Now

I penned a line, it came out wrong,
Now the plot's a silly song.
Characters dance, plot twists abound,
Improvise, oh, what a sound!

Forget the rules, let's break some hearts,
In the scene where laughter starts.
Dialogue flows like pancake batter,
Who needs a plan when jokes are fatter?

Cue the penguin, cue the cat,
This stage is wild, imagine that!
Ad-libbing lines, who knows the score?
In this script, there's always more.

As the curtain rises and falls with glee,
I'm the actor, and so are we.
With every laugh, the moment's loud,
In the chaos, we're all proud.

Foundations of the Human Spirit

I'm digging deep, found a cat,
Thought I'd find wisdom, imagine that!
Shovels ready, spirits high,
Who knew deep thoughts could sigh?

Concrete dreams poured in a mold,
But quickly freeze, I'm feeling bold.
Sloppy work, yet smiles still grow,
A foundation of fun, don't you know?

Mix and blend, let's bake a cake,
Layer of giggles, for goodness' sake!
If it tips, we'll laugh it off,
Join the party, grab a scoff!

In the chaos, joy takes root,
Building castles from this loot.
With each crack, more love will sprout,
Foundations strong, of this, no doubt.

Tapestry of Unfinished Thoughts

I wove a thread, it's quite the mess,
Colors clash, but who'd guess?
Knots tied tight, but smiles still gleam,
In this fabric, I stitch a dream.

Patterns twist, and edges fray,
Who needs rules in the creative play?
With every loop, a story spun,
A tapestry woven in quirky fun.

Sewing hope into every seam,
Embroidered laughs, not as they seem.
The more I stitch, the more I see,
This artwork grows as bold as me.

So thread that needle, pull it tight,
In this fabric, we find delight.
A tapestry of thoughts so free,
Unfinished dreams, just let them be.

Between the Plan and the Reality

I made a grand plan, oh so bright,
But the universe chuckled, 'Not tonight!'
Doodles in margins, chaos balloons,
My roadmap's lost somewhere with spoons.

Reality's like a kitten in a tree,
It climbs with such grace, but then drops, whee!
Every step forwards seems to take ten back,
Yet here I am, still riding this track.

I thought I'd be wise with a map and a guide,
But I'm more like a toddler, all wide-eyed and fried.
Building great castles with just a few blocks,
Only to trip over flip-flops and clocks.

Yet laughter erupts in this quirky parade,
For every wrong turn, new adventures are made.
So here's to the plans that go right out the door,
And the giggles they bring as we venture for more.

The Workshop of Wistful Whispers

In a workshop of dreams, I tinker away,
With thoughts like a jigsaw, in disarray.
I glue my ambitions with tape and some hope,
While my coffee pot bubbles, and dreams cope.

My mentor's a parrot with feathers so bright,
Squawking wisdom at mornings and late into night.
'You can use a spoon, or maybe a fork!'
But I can't even find where my hammer's been stored.

Blueprints of joy are scattered like crumbs,
I trip over failures, and oh, how it hums.
Yet painting my vision with strokes of delight,
Feels like crafting a sunbeam on a chilly night.

So I'll whittle and sketch in this curious place,
Where laughter and chaos help dreams find their space.
And though I might stumble, I'll keep making noise,
For creation's sweet magic is wrapped up in joys.

Navigating Life's Rough Draft

I drafted a map for this journey of mine,
But the GPS glitched, said, 'Take a recline!'
Detours and potholes, oh what a delight,
Each misadventure's another funny fright.

I planned a straight path, but found a roundabout,
With squirrels for traffic and no sign of a route.
I scribble my gags in the margin with flair,
While the universe grins at my clumsy affair.

A storm of confusion, a sprinkle of fun,
Each chapter unfolds, 'til the chaos is done.
My prose may be messy, my metaphor's vague,
But laughter's the glue that holds together this gig.

So here's to the stories, both wild and serene,
Where mistakes are the plot twists, and life's evergreen.
I'll keep navigating with a wink and a jest,
For the rough drafts of life are what I love best.

Sketches of Aspirations

With a crayon in hand, I draw future scenes,
But my art looks more like some hungry ravines.
I sketch grand ambitions, then splatter with ink,
And the paper, it sighs, 'Oh, what do you think?'

Dreams take their shapes like a pancake's high flip,
Though some land on faces; that's part of the trip.
I scribble my wishes on napkins and notes,
And hope that my destiny isn't on boats.

Each doodle and dot is a chance to create,
While my cat thinks my canvas is just his estate.
So I twist my aspirations with laughter and cheer,
Add sparkles and giggles, and call it, 'My year!'

In this gallery of mishaps, each line tells a tale,
Of the glittering moments and times when I fail.
With sketches of happiness, in colors so grand,
I embrace the weirdness at the heart of my plan.

A Mosaic of Unfinished Ideas

My vision's like a jigsaw, pieces all mislaid,
I'm trying to be Picasso, with crayons I have swayed.
Each plan is just a doodle, a sketch upon the floor,
While my cat critiques my work, he's always wanting more.

Dreams are like my laundry, they pile up day by day,
Some bright and colorful, others just fade away.
Yet I laugh at this puzzle, as I search for a few parts,
Because in this grand collage, I'm collecting all my arts.

Navigating the Unknown Path

I wander through the forest, with maps that make me sigh,

I swear I saw a signpost, but it was just a fly.
Oh, the trails are tangled, like my earphones in my bag,
But every twist and turn gives a new thought to brag.

With GPS malfunctioning, I take a different route,
Finding magic in the wrong turns, that's what it's about.
A squirrel waves me forward, a bird gives me a shout,
Each misstep is a giggle, as I figure it all out.

The Workshops of Possibility

Welcome to my workshop, it's chaos all around,
I'm assembling my dreams with a hammer and a sound.
The glue is quite stubborn, the paint is splattered wide,
But each laugh is a victory, and I take it in stride.

I've got tools for the future, some are rusty, some are new,

With every failed attempt, I learn just what to do.
Today I made a rocket, it flew right to my yard,
Now I'm building a doghouse, because life can be so hard!

Crafting Meaning in the Chaos

In my kitchen of madness, ingredients collide,
Whipping eggs with laughter, as the dough takes a ride.
The recipe's a riddle, it calls for zest and glee,
While I just toss in sprinkles, I'll eat it all for free.

With flour on my forehead, I'm battling some mess,
Creating something edible, though maybe not the best.
Yet in this crazy kitchen, I find joy in the stir,
After all, it's just some frosting, and I'm the best of her!

The Constant Horizon

I chase the sun with a sandwich in hand,
But it ducks behind clouds—oh, isn't that grand?
My GPS says I'm still on the way,
To where, I'm not sure, but hey, it's a play!

I tie my shoes, pretend I can run,
But trip over thoughts that weigh a ton.
The finish line shouts, "Who needs a date?"
It winks and says, "You're running too late!"

With laughter that echoes through space and time,
I might be lost, but I'm still in my prime.
Who knew this journey could be so absurd?
Like a squirrel on a skateboard—got that, not a bird!

So dance with the shadows and spin with the light,
For every misstep makes everything bright.
The constant horizon is just a big tease,
But I'll keep on skipping, and do it with ease!

Shades of Tomorrow on the Canvas

A brush in one hand, a donut in the other,
I paint my dreams, but the colors start to stutter.
The canvas says, "Wait! Not that shade!"
I sigh and chuckle, feeling quite played.

I smudge my creation with frosting galore,
What's that? A masterpiece? I'm not quite sure.
Yet every stroke is a story untold,
Even if it looks more like mold!

I frame it all silly, with glittery flair,
Who knew such chaos could brighten the air?
Each shade a memory, each mishap a song,
In the gallery of whacky, where all belong.

Tomorrow calls gently with shades yet to see,
But today's a party, so please stay with me!
My palette's a riot, a jumbled delight,
As we paint the fun over absurdness tonight!

Whispers of Dreams Yet to Culminate

In the quiet of night, my dreams take flight,
Like marshmallows dancing, all fluffy and light.
They whisper sweet secrets, lighter than air,
"Just start with a cookie, and go anywhere!"

I scribble my plans on a napkin cliché,
And wonder if pizza might lead the way.
My aspirations stack like a tower of cheese,
Wobbling gently, just trying to please.

A thought bubble floats, with a giggle or two,
Why not be a llama? I'd look fab in blue!
It struts through my mind, with a wiggle and sway,
Though my goals may be murky, it makes my day.

So here's to the whispers, the hopes all unfurl,
To the journeys still tangled within a swirl.
We'll laugh at the chaos, let it dance in the night,
For every wild dream is a reason to write!

The Palette of Endless Endeavors

With a splash of orange and a wink of green,
I mix up my hopes—oh, what a scene!
Endless endeavors swirl like a fright,
And I giggle aloud at my jumbled delight.

Each project a puzzle, a riddle to solve,
Like finding the TV remote every time it dissolves.
But the laughter that bubbles up like a drink,
Makes the chaos a party, more fun than you'd think!

So I doodle a dragon with googly eyes,
Sprinkle on confetti, and then loudly advise:
"Take risks like a toddler on a wobbly bike,
For the road to success is paved with the strike!"

With brushes in hand, may we color away,
The palette of futures unfolds in play.
So grab your supplies—let's make some noise,
After all, it's the journey that brings us the joy!

Composing Life's Overture

With every note, we make a sound,
Chasing laughter that knows no bounds.
A symphony of ups and downs,
In this concert, wear your crowns.

Juggling goals like flaming batons,
Tripping over our own tomfoolery.
We plan a masterpiece, and yet,
End up with a strange kind of stew.

Crayons in hand, we doodle life,
Sketching dreams through joy and strife.
Each line a giggle, each curve a chance,
To dance like we forgot our pants.

So here's to the brilliant misfit crew,
Conducting chaos, oh, who knew?
The overture of clumsy glee,
Is the greatest show we could ever see.

The Hidden Blueprints of the Heart

In my heart, there's a tangled mess,
Blueprints scribbled, no more, no less.
A sticky note says, 'Try something new,'
While another one shouts, 'What's with the stew?'

With highlighters bright, we mark our way,
Through laughter and mishaps, every day.
Plans gone rogue, like a cat in a tree,
Where's the instruction manual, I plea?

Twists and turns with a wink and a smile,
Detours and side quests, oh, they're worth the while.
Found a treasure, but lost my shoe,
Who needs a path when you've got this view?

Through tangled maps and scattered parts,
The beauty lies in our wild hearts.
So may the blueprints burst and fly,
In joyful chaos, we'll reach the sky.

Dreams in Flux

Like balloons that float and sometimes pop,
Dreams shift and sway, on a lollipop.
With every gust, they take a new route,
Bouncing around, like a wild hen's clout.

A trampoline park of hopes and schemes,
We leap and crash, fueled by our dreams.
A jigsaw puzzle with missing pieces,
Rearranging chaos, that never ceases.

In this carnival of quirky plans,
We juggle wishes with sticky hands.
Cotton candy clouds, we chase with glee,
As our visions whirl like a crazy bee.

So embrace the swirl, let it beguile,
With every flip, you'll see the style.
In the merry go-round of 'what will be,'
We'll giggle and spin, carefree and free.

The Template of Transformation

With scissors and tape, we craft our fate,
Cutting and pasting, oh, what a state!
This template speaks in a funny tone,
As we wear mismatched socks, oh the throne!

A recipe book of wrong and right,
Stirring up laughs, what a wild sight.
With every layer, the colors dance,
Our transformation unfolds at a glance.

In this workshop of curious fate,
Sawdust and giggles pile up at the gate.
We build and break, invent and surprise,
Chasing our dreams with a twinkle in our eyes.

So here's to the project, a true delight,
Crafting our lives with humor in sight.
With every turn, may we celebrate,
The template of growth, it's never too late!

Journeys in Progress

I set off with a map, oh so grand,
But Google Maps just sighed, 'What's your plan?'
With snacks in my bag and tunes in my head,
I'm zigzagging through life, hope I don't dread.

My GPS is lost, just like my sock,
It recalculates, I just want to rock!
Each detour I take, a surprise on the way,
Let's stop for some ice cream, it's a bright sunny day.

I'm collecting new stories, my suitcase a mess,
With luggage that's bursting, I still feel blessed.
A laugh or a stumble, it'll all make great tales,
Though sometimes I wonder, do I follow or bail?

With friends or alone, the road's always fine,
Each bump is a giggle, each star's a sign.
I'm still building my route, no concrete to know,
Just a journey in progress, with ups and with flow.

Trials of the Heart

I swiped right on Cupid, he missed the mark,
Now I'm dodging dates like a stroll in the park.
With a heart that is hopeful, but fragile like glass,
I laugh at the awkwardness—this too shall pass.

He brought a bouquet, but forgot it was fake,
At dinner he claimed he was gluten-free cake.
We chatted of hobbies, though I rolled my eyes,
He said he's a swimmer, but had no surprise.

My heart's on a rollercoaster, round and round,
One minute it's soaring, next pinned to the ground.
Though trials abound, I keep wearing a grin,
In the circus of dating, I just want to win!

So here's to the lovers who bumble and fumble,
I toast with a cocktail to all of the stumble.
For love is a dance, sometimes silly, though sweet,
In the trials of heart, it's a wondrous heartbeat.

The Puzzle of Existence

I'm piecing it together, this curious quest,
But where's the corner piece? It puts me to test.
Each time that I think I've got it just right,
Oh look, there's a cat! Now it's a cat fight.

With colors so bright, but edges all torn,
The box said 'smooth sailing'—I'd rather be born!
For every new piece that I think I can find,
Turns out it's a puzzle of the cat kind.

Sometimes I wonder if I'm lost in my mind,
Or just out of coffee, with no beans left to grind.
But laughter's the key to unlock every door,
And weird little puzzles, who could ask for more?

So I'll stack the pieces, despite that one hole,
Each twist and each turn dances out of control.
In the great puzzle game of this whimsical world,
I cherish the chaos, my puzzle's unfurled.

Insights from the Horizon

I climbed to the peak, what a sight to behold,
Wisdom from mountains is often retold.
But the best bit I found, shining bright at my feet,
Was the lunch that I packed—now that's a real treat!

They say to look forward, but also behind,
I looked at my sandwich—where's the mustard I find?
Yet still, as I ponder my roles in the grand,
I chuckle, oh chuckle, at the twists unplanned.

With each breath I take, the view comes alive,
The horizon is waiting, and my dreams take a dive.
Yet I trip on a rock, oh what a fine slip,
I'll laugh it off wildly, it's just part of the trip.

So here's to the insights, both silly and wise,
In the journey of seeking, oh how time flies!
Embrace every blunder, each lesson, each cheer,
For the horizon keeps shifting, it's all crystal clear.

The Constant Rebuild

I ordered a blueprint, it's on backorder,
But my builder's a cat, napping on the border.
Hammers are squeaking like they know a song,
Meanwhile, I'm scratching my head all day long.

Each wall comes with a twist, a turn quite absurd,
Like a sitcom where every joke gets deferred.
The floor plans keep changing, it's a rollercoaster,
Even the ladders seem to move a little closer.

Nails are now staples, screws turn to cheese,
And I'm still waiting for some cosmic keys.
With every new layer, my vision's still hazy,
But hey, at least the adventure is crazy!

So here's to construction on this wild ride,
Where plans are in flux, and I'll not abide.
I'll laugh at the mess as I glue it back tight,
With a smile on my face, I'll just wing it tonight!

Growing Pains of the Spirit

My heart feels like it's stretching, what's all the fuss?
Like spandex in the dryer, it's starting to rust.
Every stumble is just nature's grand joke,
While I trip over feelings; who needs a cloak?

Wisdom's a puzzle missing some parts,
Like trying to bake with all broken hearts.
Growth spurts are messy, like cake on the wall,
With frosting that whispers, 'You can have it all!'

Each bump feels like magic, or maybe a bruise,
With every odd lesson, I'm free to choose.
Embrace all the awkward, the laughs and the sighs,
'Cause the spirit's still growing; oh, how time flies!

So here's to the fun, the tadpole parade,
In this ruckus of growth, I won't be afraid.
With giggles and wiggles, I'll dance in the rain,
For every sweet struggle is never in vain!

The Canvas of Hope

With brushes all tangled and paints out of line,
I'm mixing bright colors, but nothing's a sign.
Splashes of joy, with dabs of despair,
Creating a masterpiece in mid-air!

Every stroke's a mystery, a surprise on the page,
Like my cat with a crayon, delightfully sage.
Paint drips like laughter; oh, what a scene,
My canvas is wild, it's totally green!

I've tried dots and squiggles, I've used my own toes,
Yet the vision stays fuzzy; it's one of those shows.
But hope's in the layers as I paint with my heart,
A wobbly wonder, a colorful start!

So here's to the artists with paint on their hands,
Making noise in the galleries, daring new plans.
With laughter that echoes in every bright hue,
The canvas of hope is still coming through!

Dreamscapes in Transition

My dreams are like traffic, a congested parade,
With thoughts honking loudly, in wild escapade.
Some cars are in reverse, while others speed by,
And here I am stuck, wondering why!

Building a mansion of clouds with a moat,
Really, I'm just hoping to stay afloat.
With unicorns driving my driftwood creations,
I'm shocked I haven't sparked any violations.

Every twist that I take leads to something new,
Like raining spaghetti from a luminous blue.
As I juggle my visions like fruits on a stand,
I'm chefing up dreams, didn't think I could stand!

So here's to the journey and all of its bends,
Each detour's a lesson, my imaginary friends.
With a chuckle I'll sail on this fantastical stream,
In a dreamscape of wonders, I'll dance and I'll beam!

Blueprints of Tomorrow

I sketched a plan on a napkin,
My future design, quite a laugh.
The architect? Well, that's me!
With crayons as my main staff.

I measure dreams with a ruler,
While sipping coffee, all quite absurd.
The lines never quite match up,
But hey, that's my kind of world.

I added rooms for silly moments,
And a garage for whoopee cushions.
No blueprint's ever perfect,
But mine is full of happy assumptions.

A house that grows with each sunrise,
Full of laughs and little quirks.
A framework for the absurdity,
The joy of life's playful works.

The Unfinished Road

I'm walking on a path half-paved,
With twisty turns and pothole charms.
I dodge a sign marked 'Under Repair',
With a smile as my only arms.

Mismatched shoes on my feet,
One's too big, the other's just right.
I stumble, I laugh, I carry on,
Each misstep a source of delight.

The GPS can't keep up,
It says 'Recalculating!' quite often.
Yet each detour I find exciting,
In this road trip where no one's lost 'em.

With friends and laughter beside me,
We'll create our own kind of route.
Who needs a map fully drawn?
When every turn's a joyful shout.

Dreams Under Renovation

I woke up with a plan today,
But tripped over yesterday's mess.
I'm hammering wayward wishes,
A construction zone, nonetheless.

With visions nailed to the ceiling,
I paint with colors far too bright.
My plans are more like doodles,
In the grand scheme, a pure delight.

I tried to install a new outlook,
But the instructions weren't in French.
I mixed my dreams with a twist of fate,
In this space of quirky wrench.

Renovation's a messy business,
But I laugh at what I create.
With each clumsy change I make,
I find joy in this beautiful state.

Mosaic of Meaning

Each piece I lay is slightly crooked,
A patchwork of moments gone by.
With shiny bits of glitter glue,
I craft a meaning that makes me sigh.

A tile from my childhood's laughter,
A shard from dreams I once ignored.
Mixed with puzzles of future plans,
This mosaic's fully restored.

I stick on quirks, like old receipts,
And fragments of silly old chats.
A snip from adventures, half-told,
It's a masterpiece of happy spats.

In every crack lies a story,
In every color, a sweet refrain.
This colorful chaos, vibrant and wild,
Holds the laughter through joy and pain.

Foundations Yet to Find

I built my dreams on sandy ground,
With wobbly walls, they flop around.
The blueprints drawn with crayon bright,
May need some help, or at least a light.

I tried to dig a ditch for fate,
But found a puddle – what a state!
My shovel's missing, I blame the cat,
Maybe next time I'll stick to that.

With every step, I trip and fall,
The echoes of laughter bounce off the wall.
Yet here I stand with smile so wide,
Embracing mischief like a joyful ride.

So as I climb this crazy scheme,
I'll take a moment to chase a dream.
With jumbled thoughts and mismatched shoes,
It's all a game, so what's to lose?

Mapping the Unventured Territories

I charted paths on a napkin stray,
With dotted lines that lead astray.
My compass spins like a ballerina,
Lost in wonders, oh, how serene-a!

I met a squirrel, my guide for the day,
He offered nuts instead of hay.
We followed trails of silly signs,
The kind that lead to grapevine lines.

My GPS says, "Rerouting, dude!"
But I'm still laughing, a bit less crude.
The unknown's a playground, full of cheer,
With goofy moments always near.

Each twist and turn could lead to jest,
A treasure hunt, no time for rest.
I'll waltz through life with maps askew,
In this wild ride, I'll always pursue.

Explorations in Ephemeral Moments

I caught a butterfly, bright like a dream,
But it sneezed and flew right into my cream.
A scoop of joy, with extra cringe,
These fleeting seconds, I can't binge!

I chased a rainbow through puddles and mud,
Splashing about like an overgrown bud.
But when I reached, it faded to gray,
More colorful socks were on my way!

Oh, the giggles in moments so brief,
Like finding a penny and losing belief.
I'll stitch together the laughs and the sighs,
With glittery memories that never die.

Life's a carnival, oh what a ride,
With popcorn smiles and joy as my guide.
I'll dance with time, skip the remorse,
In this merry-go-round, I'll find my course.

Unfinished Lines of the Heart

I scribble love notes with a wobbly hand,
But the ink runs out before I had planned.
With half-formed sonnets and jumbled rhymes,
I peddle my feelings like out-of-date limes.

I wrote my woes on bits of bread,
But the toaster ate them, all hope fled.
Each crusty verse tells tales of glee,
Though the punchlines left me in a spree.

With every heartbeat, a stanza breaks free,
Like a bird that forgot its own melody.
I'll gather the lines, unfinished and sweet,
In this stanza of chaos, life sounds a beat.

So here I stand, with paper and glue,
Crafting my heart, honest and true.
These unfinished lines may dance and play,
In the story of me, come what may!

Evolution of the Heart

In a world where feelings clash,
The heart evolves, oh what a bash!
With giggles and sighs, it's quite a trip,
Try not to stumble, or take a slip.

Love's like a puzzle, missing a piece,
We dance around it, searching for peace.
A twist here, a turn there, what a sight!
Who knew emotions could be so light?

Each beat an upgrade, each crush a test,
Finding the rhythm, we try our best.
With laughter in tears, a whimsical start,
Who'd think such chaos could mend a heart?

So here we go, with open minds,
Together we patch what life unwinds.
In this game of hearts, let's play our part,
Each stumble a step, in the evolution of heart.

Paving the Path Ahead

With a shovel and dreams, we start the show,
Digging our way through the highs and lows.
Each rock in the road is a lesson learned,
A quirky detour where laughter's earned.

As we pave this path with silly mistakes,
We laugh at the bumps our journey makes.
With friends by our side, we can't go wrong,
In our little parade, we sing our song.

Sometimes we twist, sometimes we slide,
But what's a good journey without a wild ride?
We're building this road, with noodles and glue,
Who knew construction could bring such a view?

So here's to the path that's never straight,
Full of surprises, laughter, and fate.
With each tiny victory, we all share a grin,
Paving the future, let the fun begin!

Navigating Uncharted Waters

With a compass in hand, we set to sea,
Navigating waves, just you and me.
The ocean's a riddle, sometimes quite mad,
But we'll steer through storms, and won't be sad.

In these uncharted waters, we skate and glide,
With fishy puns and joy as our guide.
Though the tides may shift and the winds may wail,
We smile at the chaos, we hoist our sail.

With rubber duckies and snacks galore,
We brave the currents, always wanting more.
Each splash is a giggle, a wave of delight,
As we dance on the deck under starlit night.

So here we go, on this nautical spree,
Charting our course as wild as can be.
In laughter and friendship, our boat will stay,
Navigating waters in a funnier way!

The Art of Becoming

In the studio of life, we shape and mold,
With colors of chaos, stories untold.
Each mishap a stroke on our canvas so wide,
Creating a masterpiece, with joy as our guide.

We paint with our words, and sprinkle with cheer,
Whisking up dreams, the future is near.
With a splatter of laughter, and a twist of fate,
We turn our blunders to something first-rate.

So grab a tall brush and dance on the page,
Embrace every moment, unleash the sage.
In this wacky world, we learn as we go,
The art of becoming, with room to grow.

With giggles and grins, we find our own voice,
In the art of becoming, we celebrate choice.
Each line that we sketch leads us to the fun,
Creating a symphony that's just begun!

The Scaffold of Aspirations

In a world of dreams piled high,
I'm just a builder, oh me, oh my.
With duct tape and hope on every seam,
Constructing a life, or so it seems.

My ladder's wobbly, my tools all rust,
Mixing ambition with a bit of dust.
I swing my hammer, miss the nail;
Try to stay straight, but I'm bound to fail.

The blueprints drawn with crayon or cheer,
Lucky I'm not in charge, oh dear!
With each crooked beam, I laugh and sigh,
The house of dreams will take to the sky.

But here I stand, half-built, not done,
Sunshine's a warning, not quite fun.
Yet on I go, with a twinkle and jest,
For in the mess, life's at its best.

Threading the Needle of Existence

I once tried sewing my grand design,
But I lost the thread—oh, how divine!
With needle in hand, I made a spree,
But all I got was a quilt for a bee.

Stitching together my hopes and dreams,
It's a patchwork of giggles and silly schemes.
I pricked my finger, cursed at the thread,
For in this tapestry, I'm half dead.

The fabric of life, all tangled and torn,
In the chaos, guess who was born?
An artist of mess, with fabric galore,
My masterpiece looks like a sock on the floor.

But every loop, a lesson in play,
As I stumble through this zany ballet.
So I laugh at the stitches that often mislead,
In this funny mess, I'm finally freed.

Open Roads and Uncharted Paths

I took a trip without a plan,
Wandered around like a lost tin can.
Maps upside down, signs all askew,
The GPS said, 'No, not that view!'

With socks in sandals and hair on end,
I found my way—around the bend.
Each road I traveled, a bit absurd,
Under every rock, a chicken heard.

Uncharted paths with forks galore,
Pavement? No thanks, I want some more!
I tripped on dreams and danced on doubt,
To find the gold, I found a route.

And though I'm lost, a treasure's near,
Each twist and turn brings hearty cheer.
For in each wrong step, I play the fool,
Reveling gaily, I'm making my school.

The Continuous Quest

I set out searching for the holy grail,
With a map that led me to a giant snail.
A quest to conquer whatever I seek,
But all I found was a muddy creek.

My compass spins like a trained ballet,
Is it north I'm going? Who can say?
With each misstep, I add to the tale,
Waving to cows, I'll never derail.

Through valleys of socks and fields of cheese,
I ask the daisies, 'What's next, please?'
One flower chuckled, 'Just find some bliss,'
So I stopped to dance, clutching my list.

Now my quest's less about winning the prize,
More about laughter and loud, silly sighs.
For in every stumble and silly jest,
I find that wandering is also a quest.

Foundations of a New Dawn

My plans were bold, like a lion's roar,
But lunch calls louder; I explore!
Nailed some dreams to the very wrong tree,
Now squirrels laugh, and they mock me.

The blueprint's stuck in a dramatic twist,
Turns out my coffee cup's the main gist.
Sketching my fate in crayon with flair,
But it's still a mess—I'll fix it with care.

How to build castles when I can't find the sand?
A shovel? I thought it was a band!
The workers are napping, and I've lost my spark,
Maybe I'll just embrace the quirk in the dark.

Tomorrow I'll rise, with glitter and glue,
Construct a big dream that's shiny and new.
With laughter and giggles, I'll draft and I'll play,
After all, who needs plans anyway?

Fragments of Hope

Chasing bright stars with bubble gum dreams,
But my shoelace tripped me—oh, how it screams!
Collecting my fragments, like jigsaw puzzle pieces,
Realized my plan's full of silly recesses.

Every sunrise smells like burnt toast,
Yet, every bite lets my courage boast.
Got a map to nowhere, but hey, that's alright,
At least I packed snacks for this random flight.

The future's a riddle, with puzzles galore,
But I brought extra socks, so who's keeping score?
Juggling hopes like balloons in the sky,
If one pops, I'll still wave a cheerful goodbye.

With a tumble and laugh, I'll take on the day,
Life's just a game, with confetti to play.
So here's to the chaos, let's dance in the rain,
Embrace all the nonsense, and break every chain!

The Quest for Wholeness

An epic quest for sanity, or so I thought,
Got lost in the maze that my brain never bought.
Maps bring confusion, a GPS fails,
Every turn leads to squirrelly gales.

Hunting for wholeness in crumbs of delight,
Found a pizza slice that was just out of sight.
Pizza's a circle; so, I'm almost complete,
But my diet plan said—'surrender to defeat.'

I gathered my friends in this curious quest,
Gave them all roles; they laughed as guests.
We're knights, we're jesters, in a castle of cheese,
And all my insecurities giggle with ease.

So let's raise our glasses filled up with some cheer,
To finding our wholeness—it's wonderfully clear.
Though it's messy and funny, let joy lead the way,
With laughter and friendship, I'll win this play!

Echoes of Aspirations

When aspirations come with rubbery feet,
  They wiggle and dance, never stay neat.
I wrote all my wishes on a paper boat,
  But a gust of wind made my hopes float.

Whispers of dreams in the windy night air,
  Echo of laughter, no worries or care.
With a trowel in hand, I dig for some fun,
  Even at sunset, the show's just begun.

A compass that points to the snacks in my pack,
  I'll wander forever; there's no need to hack.
My echoing ambitions are quirky, it's true,
  But I'm building a castle, one fun brick or two.

So here's to the dreams that zigzag and sway,
  They may lead me astray, but hey, that's the play.
With a giggle and twirl, I'll chase every sound,
  In this echoing world, the joy can be found!

In Pursuit of a Flickering Flame

Chasing dreams like a butterfly,
With a net made of spaghetti,
I stumble, fall, and laugh aloud,
In this circus of the steady.

Waking up feels like a heist,
Coffee's my partner in crime,
I search for meaning in my wardrobe,
Only to find mismatched rhyme.

My plans are like a sock puppet,
All dressed up but hard to speak,
I zigzag through the bumpy roads,
Maybe chaos is a leak.

So here I am, all tangled up,
A jester in my own grand show,
Constructing visions with no blueprint,
Laughing as my dreams overflow.

The Architecture of Existence

Building castles with crayon bricks,
A blueprint found in last night's snack,
With giggles as my only tool,
I bring my childlike dreams intact.

Walls that wiggle, doors that squeak,
A window made of cobweb threads,
My architecture's quite absurd,
As laughter dances in my head.

I lay the stones of silly thoughts,
A roof of jokes, a floor of glee,
Each beam echoes with a pun,
And blueprints filled with jubilee.

Though my designs may sway and bow,
I build in whimsy, brick by brick,
In every crack, a laugh is found,
In this project, love's the trick.

Under the Hammer

With a hammer in my clumsy grip,
I swing and miss, oh what a sight,
Each nail a giggle, each thud a cheer,
The construction site feels just right.

I measure dreams with measuring spoons,
The architect of my own delight,
As blueprints fly like paper planes,
And laughter guides my heart's limelight.

Chasing shadows that tease the light,
I build my hopes on stilts of jest,
With every swing, I laugh and trip,
A clumsy builder, but never stressed.

Under the hammer, I find my rhythm,
Each bang a chuckle, each mishap gold,
Constructing magic with scraps of joy,
In this bouncy house, I am bold.

Dreams Take Shape

In the land where dreams can dance,
I twirl with thoughts like cotton candy,
Shapes are goofy, colors wild,
In this funhouse, oh so dandy.

I trace my hopes in silly loops,
With crayons bright, I leave no mark,
Each stroke a trip, each hue a laugh,
As I craft joy from every spark.

The forms are strange, but that's the fun,
A jellybean heart with wings that flop,
Hopping through the magic flow,
Building dreams that never stop.

So grab your brush, let's paint the sky,
With polka dots and zigzag lines,
In this world of funny shapes,
Creativity forever shines.

Foundation Stones of the Heart

Lay the bricks with love and smiles,
Each stone a giggle, each laugh a gift,
Mortar made of kindness and fun,
In this heart, my spirits lift.

Constructing joy in every crack,
With layers of whimsy, strong and bright,
I measure happiness in chuckles,
And build my dreams to reach new heights.

Foundations shake, yet stand so tall,
With silly puns as sturdy beams,
Together we can raise the walls,
Our laughter echoes through the dreams.

For in this world of endless play,
With every stone, my heart does sing,
Under construction, always bright,
Building joy in everything.

The Journey of Discovery

I set off with a map so grand,
But somehow it slipped from my hand.
With coffee stains and doodles bright,
I wander left when I should go right.

Each sign I see, a riddle or quiz,
A squirrel named Bob is now my whiz.
We chat about dreams and pies we crave,
As I take the wrong turn on this crazy wave.

My GPS is lost in deep thought,
While I ponder the rounds I never fought.
Yet laughter spills like a bubbling stew,
Who knew that fun was my greatest view?

So here's to trips with goofy twists,
Where missteps turn to treasure lists.
The maps are jokes, and the roads are sly,
I'm giggling along, waving good-bye.

Threads of Uncertainty

I tried to weave a blanket fine,
But tangled yarn is my design!
Each stitch a question, each knot a thought,
Who knew crafting could leave me caught?

Patterns shift like socks in socks,
My puzzle's missing essential blocks.
I toss the thread, let chaos reign,
In this knitted mess, I can't complain.

A scarf of dreams, but what's the use,
When it's more like a lopsided noose?
Yet in the mess, I find my cheer,
With every loop, a smile, sincere.

So here's to threads that refuse to lay,
To patterns wild in a zany way.
In this fabric of life, I still explore,
Each stumble a laugh, who could want more?

Sketches of the Soul

I took my pencil to sketch my fate,
But doodles of cats have sealed that state.
With every line, my dreams parade,
In wobbly circles, my plans invade.

I drew a house but added a tree,
Where squirrels dance, just wild and free.
My canvas, a collage of silly cheer,
As I scribble away, my focus unclear.

A unicorn here, a donut over there,
With wild ideas flying in the air.
My masterpiece? A mural of fun,
With colors splashed under the sun.

So here's to sketches with crazy hues,
To stories told in rainbow views.
In the gallery of dreams, I'll take my stroll,
Each laugh a stroke, every smile a goal.

Wanderlust of the Mind

I sail on clouds, with popcorn for sails,
Chasing my dreams through whimsical trails.
The stars are my guide, but oh, how they twirl,
In a mad dash of thoughts, my brain gives a whirl.

Adventures soar in a fizzy delight,
With dragons and pizza stacked eight feet high.
I bounce through realms, in my jammies still,
As giggles echo with every thrill.

In the circus of thoughts, I am the clown,
With mismatched shoes as I tumble down.
Yet joy paints the skies, with colors galore,
In this wacky land, who could ask for more?

So here's to the wanderers, lost in the play,
With dreams painted bright, come what may.
May our minds forever roam and glide,
In this funny quest, let's take a ride!

Revelations of an Architect's Heart

My plans are quite ambitious, oh dear,
Yet each brick feels like a disappearing sphere.
Blueprints in crayon, a site full of glee,
Constructing my dreams, or just a teetering tree?

Every room's a puzzle, a whimsical dance,
Walls lean left, as if caught in a trance.
The roof's gone rogue, does it want to take flight?
Oh well, let it soar! It's a bird, what a sight!

Windows are winking, they giggle and sway,
With curtains that twirl, oh what a display!
I laugh with the beams that creak and they sigh,
This house might just wander right up to the sky!

But who's keeping score in this charming charade?
My plans may be silly, but I'm not dismayed!
An architect's heart is a comedy show,
Constructing a legend, no need for a pro!

Expanding the Portrait of Existence

With colors of chaos, I splatter and splash,
Each stroke's a reminder that time's gone in a flash.
Canvas of laughter, of dreams yet to find,
Life's like a puzzle, though pieces unwind.

Paintbrushes wobble, creating a mess,
Oh look, that's a chicken! No wait, that's a dress!
Swirling in circles, twirling with grace,
My portrait of being's a delightful disgrace!

Who knew a sunbeam could look like a noodle?
Or shadows could dance like a wild little poodle?
In this gallery crazy, each art style's a fling,
I'm a masterpiece, or just a 'thing' on a string?

Framed in the funny, I pucker and pout,
With each brush of bliss, I'm still figuring out.
An artist's ambition, a whimsical jest,
In this colorful chaos, I'm simply a guest!

Shadows and Silhouettes of Tomorrow

Oh look at the shadows, they play hide and seek,
Trying to sneak past the light with a squeak.
Dancing like ninjas, all silent, yet spry,
What are they plotting? A leap to the sky?

The silhouettes giggle, with hats made of flair,
They tiptoe and twirl, without a single care.
A gathering jest, both ridiculous and grand,
Future's a party, the bait is well planned.

Tomorrow's a riddle, wrapped tight in a bow,
But me? I just laugh, with my flashlight aglow.
Life's an odd circus, with clowns that confound,
I'll juggle my dreams, make them bouncy and round!

With no map or guide, let's wander and play,
In shadows and silhouettes, we'll find our own way.
A ticket to giggles, an entry to fun,
Tomorrow's a carnival, and oh, we've just begun!

The Tapestry Unraveling

Oh what a mess, this tapestry of mine,
Threads caught in laughter, a graphical line.
Stitches of chaos, in colors so bold,
This fabric of nonsense is pure treasure gold!

With every loose thread, a tale's coming free,
A sock from who knows where, or maybe a bee!
Intricate patterns, I weave on a whim,
The fluff of my thoughts, they start to get grim.

But wait! There's a yarn that tickles my nose,
A twist of adventure, as the laughter grows.
Each unraveling moment becomes quite the art,
A tapestry tangled, but warm to the heart!

So bring on the mishaps, I'll embrace the fluke,
With laughter as glue, and joy as the hook.
Life's such a quilt, in a colorful range,
Unraveling my story, how could it not change?

Pilgrimage of Intent

I set out with a map, oh so bright,
But every turn was quite a fright.
I tripped on dreams, fell in a ditch,
Guess my compass is a little rich.

With every step, I lose my way,
Maybe I'll just sleep today.
The path's unclear, I hear a laugh,
Is that success or just my gaff?

I asked a pro, he shrugged and said,
"Follow your shoes, not your head!"
So here I am, and oh what fun,
Still wandering, but at least I run!

Each stumble's a lesson, that's what they say,
Can I get a break, or just more play?
I'll march ahead, with a grin and jest,
Finding joy in this less-than-perfect quest.

Navigating the Unfinished Symphony

My notes are scattered, like leaves in a storm,
I sing off-key, but it feels like warm.
The melody's missing, where could it be?
Oh wait, found it—hiding in my tea!

Harmonies clash like socks in the wash,
Every attempt feels a bit posh.
Crescendos pop like balloons in the night,
Yet I dance on, fueled by delight.

I wrote a sonnet, but it looked like spam,
Critics chuckled, "What a jam!"
But I'll keep playing, come rain or shine,
This quirky tune is absolutely mine!

Rhythms change, but my spirit stays,
In every note, I'll find new ways.
Confusion reigns—I just laugh and spin,
For every flop, there's a chance to grin.

The Sculptor's Dilemma

I chisel away with a hopeful heart,
This block of stone, my works of art.
But with each tap, it crumbles so nice,
Is it a statue or just a slice?

I asked a wise man, he grinned and said,
"Just try to create what's in your head!"
But my head's a mess, like a puzzle unsolved,
These pieces roll off, can't get involved!

I mold a hand, but it looks like a foot,
Community laughs, but I still pursue.
"Keep at it!" they cheer, while snickering loud,
My shrine's a circus, but I'm still proud!

In every flaw, there's beauty's embrace,
A twist of humor lines every trace.
One day I'll finish, or maybe I won't,
But here's my art—let's all have a jaunt!

Mapping the Heart's Terrain

I drew up a map of my feelings so vast,
But it led me right to a field of grass.
X marks the spot, but I lost the key,
Who needs GPS when you're feeling free?

My compass spins, it's a bit confused,
And I'm left wondering what I've refused.
Fuelled by laughter, I wander around,
Each laugh's a treasure, forever unbound.

I reached a fork where dreams collide,
Left for comfort, right for a ride.
I chose the middle, tripped on a shoe,
But oh what a journey! What else is new?

The heart's a maze, full of quirks and turns,
Lessons are planted, it's wisdom that burns.
With every misstep, I cheer and dance,
Embracing the chaos's wild romance.

www.ingramcontent.com/pod-product-compliance
Lightning Source LLC
Chambersburg PA
CBHW051656160426
43209CB00004B/916